I am a Rainbow

A Children's Guide to the

Sarah Smid & Amanda Cottrell

Library of Congress Cataloging-in-Publication Data Available

ISBN: 9781795658652
Published by Art Mindfulness and Creativity
www.artmindfulnessandcreativity.com

To all of the little lights! Shine brightly my dears and Ella of course!

To Zoe
HAPPY BIRTHDAY!

LOVE
E-ni-ci ♡

I am a rainbow. My body is filled with light.

Just like a prism, when a light shines through me, a beautiful rainbow can be seen.

This special rainbow inside of me tells me how my body, mind and spirit are feeling and connecting.

The parts of my rainbow are called the chakras. Knowing how this rainbow works can tell me when something is not right. There are seven main chakras in my body to guide me, heal me and help me find balance.

At the base of my body sits the red part of my rainbow. It is known as the root chakra. Just like a tree has roots, my root chakra grounds me and tells me how I am connecting to the world around me.

When my root chakra is balanced, I feel calm and supported. I am able to make good choices.

When my root chakra is imbalanced, I feel unsafe, insecure, doubtful and fearful. Sometimes it might be hard for me to make good choices, especially when I'm upset.

To balance and heal the root chakra, I can do different activities to help me feel more connected. This might include spending some time in nature, or doing grounding exercises like yoga or meditation. Carrying stones like hematite, bloodstone, or red jasper can also help me heal and find balance.

My second chakra
sits just below my
belly button. It is an
orange colour, and
is known as the
sacral chakra. It tells
me about my
emotions, including
how I feel about
myself and others. It
also helps me with
my creativity.

When my sacral chakra is balanced, I feel positive, confident, and whole. I am able to create freely.

When my sacral chakra is imbalanced, I can sometimes have big, out of control feelings that last a long time, or sometimes feel nothing at all; like emptiness.

To balance and heal the sacral chakra, I can meditate while picturing a bright orange light surrounding my body like a blanket. It can also be healing to take a bath or spend time in or near the water, like a river, stream or lake. Carrying stones like citrine, carnelian or orange calcite can also help me heal and find balance.

Just above my belly button sits the yellow part of my rainbow. It is known as the solar plexus chakra. It tells me about my mind and thoughts, and keeps me mentally aware and strong.

When my solar plexus chakra is balanced, I feel smart. I know who I am and what I want. I am full of clarity.

When my solar plexus chakra is imbalanced, I feel out of control and might want to try to control too much. I sometimes find planning and decision making difficult, like my brain is fuzzy.

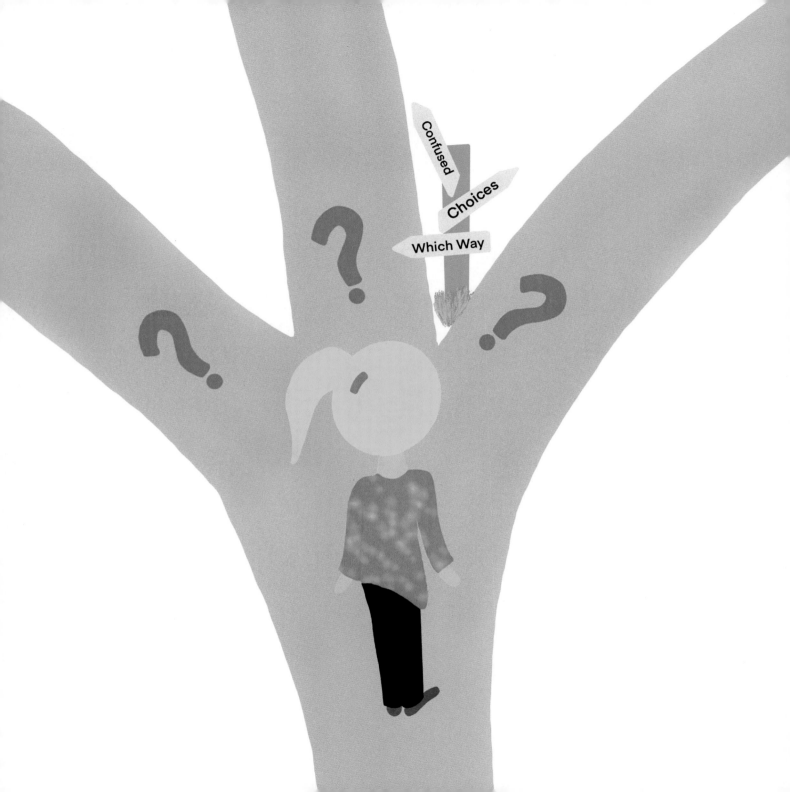

To balance and heal my solar plexus chakra, I can move my body. Doing activities like dancing, yoga or meditation are helpful for this chakra. Carrying stones like amber, golden calcite or sunstone can also help me heal and find balance.

Right in the middle of my chest sits the green part of my rainbow, but sometimes people see pink, and that's okay too! This is known as the heart chakra. It tells me how I love myself and others.

When my heart chakra is balanced,
I feel peace, love and acceptance
for myself and those around me.

When my heart chakra is imbalanced, I feel shy, lonely and sometimes cranky. I might also find it hard to forgive people when they hurt my feelings.

To balance and heal the heart chakra, I can spend time with someone I love, like a family member or pet, and maybe have a snuggle with them. I can take care of myself by doing things that make me happy and calm. Carrying stones like rose quartz or green aventurine can also help me heal and find balance.

The blue part of my rainbow sits where my throat is. This is why it is called the throat chakra. It helps me with self-expression and allows me to speak my truth.

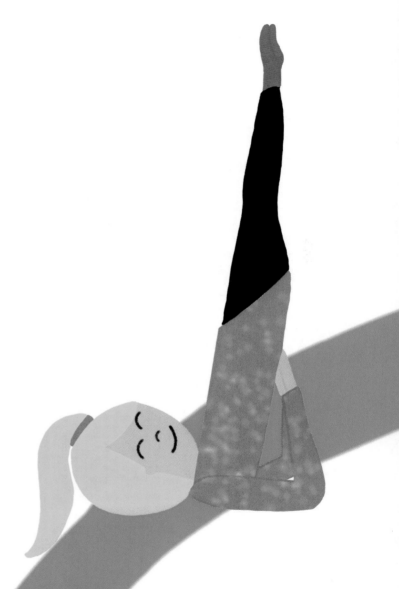

When my throat chakra is balanced, I feel like I can express myself easily. I am loyal and truthful.

When my throat chakra is imbalanced, I can feel anxious and misunderstood by others. I may feel the need to hide my "true self".

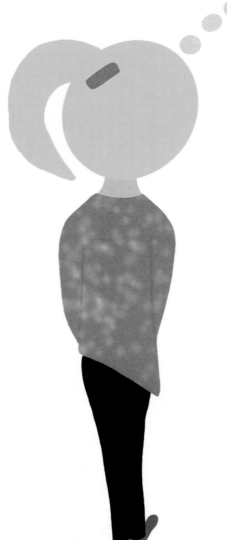

To balance and heal the throat chakra, I can sing my favourite songs, or write down things I may want to say, but can't. Laughter can also be a powerful tool in clearing blockages in this area. Carrying stones like blue calcite, sodalite or lapis lazuli can help heal and bring balance to the throat chakra.

In the middle of my forehead sits the indigo or violet part of my rainbow. It is known as the third eye chakra. My third eye chakra is responsible for my imagination, intuition, self-awareness and wisdom.

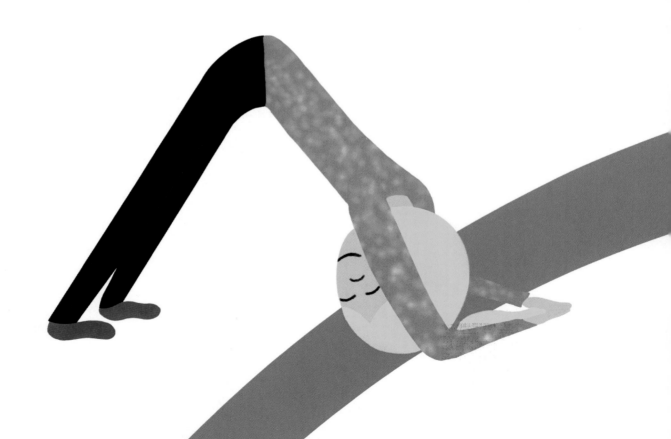

When my third eye chakra is balanced, both my thinking brain and my creative brain are able to work together. I am able to see and reflect on the world around me more clearly.

When my third eye chakra is imbalanced, I might not trust myself or listen to my gut instincts. I might not be open to the ideas of others, and can be stubborn.

To balance and heal the third eye chakra, I can do mindfulness practices like deep breathing or following a guided meditation. Sunlight also helps clear blockages in this chakra, so spending time outside is important. Carrying stones like kyanite, labradorite and amethyst can help open this chakra, giving me healing and balance.

At the top of my head sits my last chakra. It is the purple part of my rainbow, but sometimes people see white or gold, and that's okay too! This is called my crown chakra. It is responsible for connecting with my higher self.

When my crown chakra is balanced, I feel blissful and complete. I am aware of my own self and am able to selflessly focus on the well-being of others.

When my crown chakra is imbalanced, everyday activities can feel difficult and I might feel "out of it" or "blah". I don't have a good connection or awareness of myself.

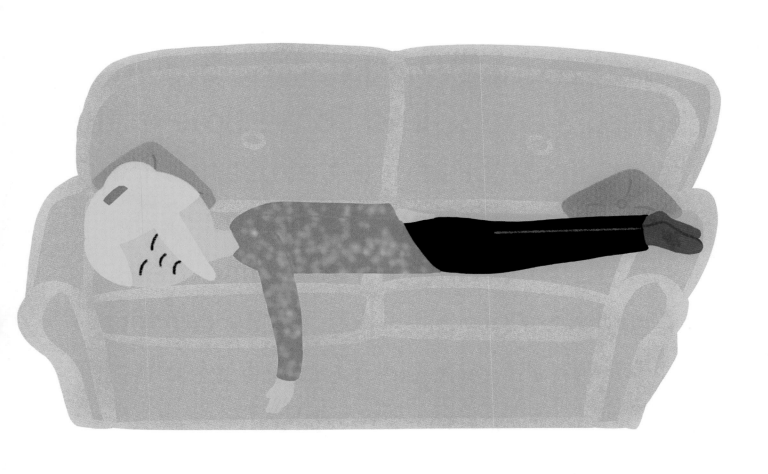

To balance and heal the crown chakra, I can spend some time in the fresh air or practice belly breathing. Doing yoga, meditation or other mindful practices can also help. Carrying stones like snow quartz, selenite or purple fluorite can help me heal and find balance.

Healing and balancing all of the parts of our rainbows takes time and practice. Just like it is important to exercise our bodies, it is important to balance the energies within it. When all of our chakras are balanced, energy is able to freely flow through them, which helps us in our day to day lives. It makes living easier, as balance has a ripple effect. When we are healed we are better able to connect to ourselves, others and the world.

Sarah has been studying energy work since 2009. She practices Reiki and crystal healing. She is an elementary school teacher who's passion is working with children with a variety of needs. Sarah lives in Calgary, Alberta.

Believe, Create, Inspire

Amanda's mission is to help people develop and explore their creative gifts through art, yoga and mindfulness. She is an author, illustrator and teacher (B.A., B.Ed.,M.Ed) Amanda lives in Calgary, Alberta with her daughter Ella.

www.artmindfulnessandcreativity.com

Made in the USA
Coppell, TX
14 March 2021

51703360R00031